Buy Me!
A Predictable Process For Poshmark Sales

Contents

Preface:

Do you want to sell fashion on Poshmark without the tedious and time-consuming process of community building, gaining thousands of followers and sharing your posts just for the slight chance of a sale like all of the other "experts" suggest? Then this is the book for you!

How do I know? Because I did it the "right" way. I followed the recommended processes. I took months to curate my version of a perfect Poshmark page and did everything I could to get followers. Sure, I got a few sales but it took a lot of effort. And then I uncovered a secret to fast forward sales!

I have developed a predictable, easy-to-follow process that leads to Poshmark sales regardless of the amount of time you've been a Posher, the number of items in your closet, the number of followers or amount of shares. All you need to get started are the Poshmark basics – a page and a listing.

If you don't a Poshmark page yet check out the free Poshmark blog. This is where you can learn the basics on how to set up a closet. Use my invitation code (GCYQW) and you will receive a $5 credit just for signing up! If you have questions about setting up your closet send me a message @mcdonss.

Got a Poshmark page? Then let's get started!

Plus, I've included two BONUS CHAPTERS that outline predictable techniques on how to get sales from new Poshers and increase your odds of getting a listing chosen as a Host Pick.

Who knows, you could be the next success story like Girl Boss, Sophia Amuroso, founder of Nasty Gal!

Check out my closet and follow me @mcdonss.

What's Love Got To Do With It?

The love for high quality fashion has catapulted Poshmark to one of the top used clothing apps. It is estimated that Poshmark hosts millions of shoppers and even more sellers. Even better for you, it is estimated that there is a sale every 2 seconds!

Poshmark's core vibe is a social tool to buy and sell used clothing. They lovingly call their members Poshers. There are Posh Parties, Follow-Me Games and a plethora of social networking opportunities to connect with others or find items you love. They recently added a Dressing Room feature as another place for Poshers to connect.

But my goal is to sell with as little effort as possible. After a few sales under my belt, I wanted to understand how I got them so I could follow the same process to get more. It appeared that there was no rhyme or reason to the sales. Which lead me to wonder, which Posh tools would get me the most sales? Could it be by gaining more followers? Sharing my listings more often?

I wanted to know the most effective way to sell more so I could only focus on tasks that directly impacted my sales. Why spend time sharing my listings if that wasn't the quickest way to a sale? But that's what all of the top Poshmark advice told me to do – share, share, share. I spent weeks sharing all of my listings resulting in a sale here and there but nothing spectacular or predictable. And I had no indication if the purchaser bought through my efforts or the purchaser simply found my listing through search.

So I took the challenge upon myself and by analyzing the process and Posher behavior, I developed a 5 step process that I've named "Have a HEART" because it focuses on how to get high quality (not quantity) hearts/likes to capture sales.

This is a process any Posher can follow. It's simple and your Poshmark statistics like number of followers, number of shares or number of closet items is absolutely irrelevant! Even if you're a beginner this process will work. All you need to start is a great Poshmark listing!

There is no random community building, sharing aimlessly or a minimum number of followers required. In fact, a by-product of this simple process is just that. Not only will you gain sales, your community base will naturally grow through this process.

If you love Poshmark sales, read on!

The Power of Love: Importance of Posh Likes

The way to sell any item is to expose an interested buyer to a product at the time the buyer is ready to make a purchase. As discussed, there are many ways to get exposure to your items on Poshmark. Gain followers and share your listings with them (in hopes they are looking at their feed…), Self-Shares, Posh Member Shares, Posh Parties and even your own Social Media Channels.

In my experience, the most powerful selling tool in Poshmark is the Like feature. Most of the time, Poshers heart/like an item they are interested to purchase. That purchase may come immediately or saved in their Like list to purchase later. So even though it's not always instant, if a Posher Likes your listing you can assume there is interest.

The key is quality Likes versus quantity of Likes, or number of Likes. If you have 100 Likes on your listing but none of them are interested buyers, the quantity is irrelevant. However, if you have 10 Likes from Poshers who are extremely interested in your listing, your chances of selling that item goes up.

Moreover, once you have quality Likes on a listing you can communicate to those Poshers in two ways:
1. Messaging Feature: You can start a conversation such as ask a Posher if they need more information about the listing.
2. Lowering Your Price: When you drop the price of a listing the Poshers who have Liked the listing will get a notification and possibly discounted shipping (typically applied if the price is dropped by 10% off the lowest historical price).

If Poshers have Liked your item, you are communicating with those who have essentially self-subscribed to your listing. You are ready for the communication, negotiating and selling to begin!

So how do you get the maximum number of quality Likes on your listings? It's simple. The **Have a HEART** Process!

The Law Of Attraction: How To Get Posh Likes

Poshmark is social in nature and with that there is a Posh etiquette that if someone shares your listing it is encouraged to share one of their listings as a sign of gratitude. While this helps with getting your listing seen by other Poshers, are they interested? Is it their size? Not likely.

But what if you can use this etiquette to your advantage to nearly guarantee quality Likes on your listings? How? By searching for similar products and harvesting those who have already shown interest in the same, or a similar listing on another Posher's page. Basically, find Poshers who have already liked a similar product and casually introduce them to your listing. They are more likely to buy especially if you have higher quality, more competitive pricing, faster shipping, discounted pricing, other products to bundle with etc.

In the following example, the listing on the left is my listing that I am trying to sell by getting quality Likes. The listing on the right is a similar listing that already had 12 Likes. Continue to the next chapter for the step-by-step process on how I introduce those who already Liked a similar listing to my listing. Since they already Liked the other listing, it's likely they will also be interested in mine.

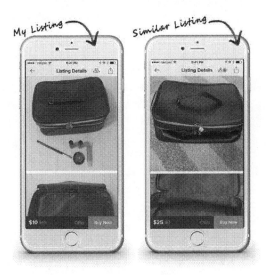

Have a HEART: Simple 5 Step Process

Follow these 5 simple steps to casually introduce your listings to Poshers who have already shown interest in similar listings. It's important to perform each step in order. The steps will become seamless once you are familiar with the process.

H = Handpick a listing that you want to target for quick sales
E = Examine similar listings price, quality, condition etc.
A = Adjust your handpicked listing to be competitive (if needed)
R = Reorganize your closet so your handpicked item is at the top
T = Target (Like/Share/Follow) those who have liked similar listings to prompt them to visit your page and Like your listing

Below is more detail on each step:

1) **Handpick** a listing from your closet that you would like to increase the chance for a sale. For your first time, consider choosing a product that is popular, easy to search for and is size agnostic. For example, a designer hand bag, jewelry or sunglasses. These are items that are very easy to find similar listings and you don't have to worry about size and style. Once you get familiar with the process, this will become easy and intuitive for any item.

2) **Examine** similar listings to understand your competition. Go to "Shop" and search by Key Word, Brand or Categories similar to your listing. Note the price, quality and condition of other listings. Search in the same size, brand and style as your product. If there aren't very many listings, broaden your search to other colors or similar brands. Note listings that are an exact match and/or have many Likes to make the following steps much quicker. I find it helpful to make a list for future reference and I've provided real scenarios in the upcoming chapters.

3) **Adjust** your handpicked listing (if needed) based on the information you observed in the previous step.
   - Add value by highlighting how your item is different than others in the headline or description
   - Adjust price (up or down) if needed to be competitive
   - If photography was better in other listings, snap a new photograph and upload it to be the cover image

Set your price at least 10% above your actual selling price. Later, if you lower your price by at least 10% each person who has Liked your item will receive a notification and potentially discounted shipping. This could lead to an instant sale once this action is triggered.

4) **Reorganize** your Poshmark Closet so your handpicked listing is one of the first 3 listings. In the next step, you will be casually introducing others to your closet and the handpicked listing so it must appear at the top of your closet.

Put other listings you want to attract attention to among the first 6 listings. The next step will get you increased traffic to your Poshmark Closet so you want your handpicked item and your other best listings to be the first thing they see. Your visitors may not take the time to scroll past the first few listings so this step is very important. Sharing items with your followers makes them appear at the top of your Poshmark Closet. You can confirm the order of your closet by exiting your closet after sharing and reentering.

5) **Target: Like / Share / Follow** Go back to the similar listings that already had Likes. Click on each Posher who liked that listing and do the following for each:
   - Like a Listing(s) in their closet
   - Follow them
   - Share a listing(s) in their closet

Repeat to all who liked similar listings. If the Posher has no items, Like/Share their profile picture and Follow them. If there are more than 11 Likes on the listing, a list will appear which makes the process much quicker. Otherwise, go one by one to each person's closet and Like a Listing, Follow them and Share a listing in their closet.

It's as simple as that! Why does the **Have a HEART** process work? Because most Poshers are going to take note of your activity on their page. Their most likely reaction will be to click on your closet and return the favor and share one of your listings or begin following you.

The magic of the **Have a HEART** process is when they do that, the target listing that they have already Liked in the past is right in front of them! They might purchase your item instantly, or Like it for future reference resulting in a quality Like for future communications and possibly discounts. They also might purchase or Like a different item in your closet, share or follow you.

All of these scenarios are advantageous and lead to predictable sales!

Next, read through actual examples to get a better understanding of the entire process.

Love Does Exist: Real Examples

Let's review actual results gained by following the **Have a HEART** process. Each example was performed on varying days of the week, varying times of the day and with a variety of products.

The ultimate goal is quality Likes and quick, predictable sales but there are also other long-term advantages because every time you follow the **Have a HEART** process you will gain Likes, shares and followers. Remember, it's not the quantity of Likes you are working for, it's quality.

Each of the scenarios provided are actual examples that show the handpicked listing, an overview of the process, a chart showing the similar products that were targeted and most importantly, the results.

Example 1: Shorts

I chose a pair of shorts for my handpicked listing and began the process on a Sunday at 4:15 p.m. by moving the listing to the top of my closet.

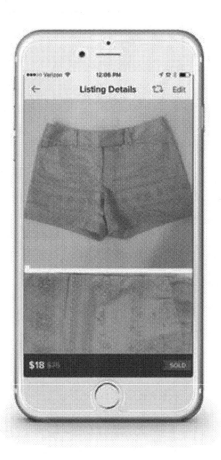

I found 9 similar listings at varying price points. Of those 9 listings, 67 Poshers had already Liked the similar listings. I followed the "Target: Like/Follow/Share" step 67 times and it took me approximately 20 minutes.

Like Product Name	Price Point	# of Likes
NWT WHBM Linen Shorts	$35	14
WHBM Shorts	$5	9
WHBM Stripe Shorts	$18	13
WHBM Shorts	$23	2
WHBM Shorts	$20	5
WHBM Shorts	$25	4
WHBM Shorts (Same)	$25	6
WHBM Shorts White Trim	$25	9
WHBM Shorts Brown	$30	5
Total # of Poshers		67

Just as I finished the process, one of the targeted Likes purchased my listing! My results were:
- **Purchase within 30 Minutes!**
- 4 Target Item Likes
- 12 Likes On Other Listings
- 23 Shares
- 38 New Followers

Example 2: Sunglasses

I chose a pair of Maui Jim Pau Hana Sunglasses for my handpicked listing and began the process on a Sunday at 12:00 p.m. by moving the listing to the top of my closet.

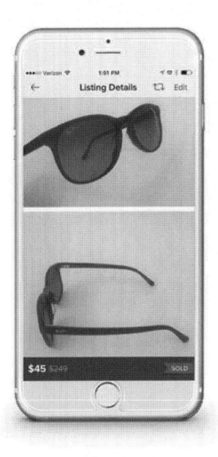

I found 2 similar listings at varying price points, both were much more expensive than my listing because they had the case included. Of those 2 listings, 45 Poshers had already liked the similar listings. I followed the "Target: Like/Follow/Share" step on all 45 Poshers who had Liked the similar listing and it took me approximately 15 minutes.

Like Product Name	Price Point	# of Likes
Pau Hana Maui Jim Sunglasses	$125	44
Authentic Maui Jim Pan Hana	$190	1
TOTAL		45

I got 6 Likes on the sunglasses within 24 hours. I sold the sunglasses to one of those 5 days later after I lowered the price and the Poshers who Liked the listing were notified.

- **Purchase within 5 Days!**
- 6 Target Item Likes
- 16 Likes On Other Listings
- 27 Shares
- 50 New Followers

Example 3: Fur Vest

I chose a Tart Fur Vest for my handpicked listing and began the process on a Saturday at 4:30 p.m. by moving the listing to the top of my closet.

I found 12 similar listings at varying price points. I found no similar listings that were the exact same product so I targeted general faux fur vests. Of those 12 listings, 97 Poshers had already Liked the similar listings. I followed the "Target: Like/Follow/Share" step on all 97 Poshers who had liked the similar listings and it took me approximately 30 minutes.

Like Product Name	Price Point	# of Likes
Miss Me Faux Fur Vest	$30	7
525 America Class Fur Vest	$60	1
Faux Fur Cable Knit Vest	$25	4
White House Black Market Faux Fur Vest	$32	5
Faux Daytrip Fur Vest by Buckle	$19	11
Rabbit Fur & Cashmere Vest	$78	2
BR Fur Vest	$30	9
Banana Republic Fur Vest	$65	3
NWT Michael Kors Faux Fur Vest	$64	26
Faux Fur Vest	$65	4
Fur Vest	$65	4
Faux Fur Vest	$55	21
TOTAL		97

I got 4 Likes on the Tart Fur Vest within 24 hours and while I haven't sold the vest, 1 of the 97 Poshers purchased 2 other items in a bundle the next day! This is why it's important to have your top listings also at the top of your closet.

- **2 Closet Items Bundled and Purchased!**
- 4 Target Item Likes
- 17 Likes On Other Listings
- 30 Shares
- 22 New Followers

Example 4: Cosmetic Bag

I chose a Lancôme cosmetic bag with samples for my handpicked listing and began the process on a Tuesday at 11:00 a.m. by moving the listing to the top of my closet.

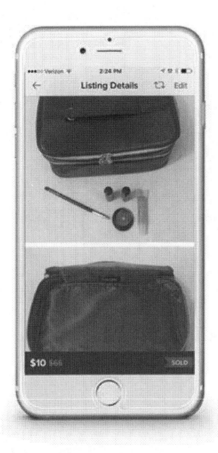

I found 9 similar listings at varying price points. Some were only the cosmetic bag and some also contained samples. Of those 9 listings, 96 Poshers had already Liked the similar listings. I followed the "Target: Like/Follow/Share" step on all 96 Poshers who had Liked the similar listings and it took me approximately 30 minutes.

Like Product Name	Price Point	# of Likes
Lancôme Travel Set	$40	2
Lancôme Raspberry Patent Cosmetic Bag	$20	12
Lancôme Black Polka Dot Cosmetic Bag	$20	9
New Lancôme Gift Set	$22	11
Bi-Facial Travel Size (4 Eye Make-up Removers)	$20	13
Lancôme 10 Piece Bundle	$45	7
NWOT Lancôme Bi-Facial Eye Make-up Remover	$10	24
Lancôme Sample Bundle with Travel Case	$15	9
Misc. 1 Like Listings		9
TOTAL		96

I got 5 Likes and gained 42 Followers within 24 hours. The cosmetic bag sold 3 weeks later.
- **Purchased within 3 Weeks!**
- 5 Target Items Likes
- 24 Likes On Other Listings
- 41 Shares
- 42 New Followers

Share The Love: You're Turn

Set a schedule and goals. While this process is predictable, it does take time and the more you do it the more results you will get. You can follow these steps anywhere you have Internet. Coffee shop? Lunch break? Train Ride? Binge watching Boss Girl on Netflix? When I spend 20-30 minutes per day on the **Have a HEART** process, I typically get a sale every 2-3 days.

Just determine the amount of time you have per day/week/month to invest in performing these Poshmark short-cuts. The amount of time each action takes will vary, the more you do it the quicker you will be. But below are some basic time expectations.

1) **Have a HEART Process – Posher Liked Similar Listings:**
   15-20 Minutes per 50 targets
   25-30 Minutes per 100 targets

   - Finding similar listings with a large number of "Likes" will make the process much faster.
   - Practice makes perfect! The more you do the **Have a HEART** process, the quicker you will become.
   - On average for my examples, following the **Have a HEART** process for 100 similar products results in 5-10 quality Likes on my handpicked item.

2) **New Poshers – Likely to be interested in Buying versus Selling**
   5 Minutes per 25 New Poshers

3) **Host Pick – Increase Odds to have your Listing a Host Pick**
   5 Minutes (Based on 4 Posh Parties per day and multiple hosts per party)

Conclusion:
To get predictable sales on Poshmark, you have to understand the basics. If a product you are targeting isn't selling, examine other products that are selling and determine if your item need to be adjusted. Then follow the **Have a HEART** process again.

In addition, some items are more likely to sell quicker than others so you have to be patient and keep targeting likely buyers.

Visit the Poshmark Blog at any time to get great tips on how to set-up an amazing closet. Or follow me @mcdonss and ask me questions at anytime.

The more strategic you can be, the more you will sell! Good luck!

Bonus Chapter: How To Get Sales from New Poshers

I have found that many of my purchases come from New Poshers who don't have any listings. There are many theories as to why, but I think the most simple and logical explanation is that they are likely more focused on shopping than selling.

Using the same philosophy as the **Have a HEART** process, you can target new Poshers by casually introducing them to your closet and listings.

And it's simple!

1) Click on "Shop"

2) Scroll Down to "Discover People"

3) Click on "New People"

4) Click on "Just Joined"
   (Be sure your size is included in the "Filters" pull-down menu if you want to target people with a similar size)

5) Click on each name and perform the "Target: Like/Follow/Share" step of the **Have a HEART** process.
   (Since these are new Poshers, they may not have listings. Like and Share their profile picture if they have no listings)

As described in previous chapters, your activity on their page and the Poshmark Share etiquette will likely attract their attention enough to view your closet.

This can lead to quality Likes, quick sales, followers and more! And there is little time investment. I have found that I can target 25-30 new Poshers in 5 minutes. Perhaps follow this process while enjoying that morning cup of coffee each morning? Or on the train ride home after work?

Bonus Chapter: How To Increase Odds of Being a Host Pick

There are typically 4 Posh Parties per day that are announced the day prior. If you're not familiar with Host Parties, check out the free Poshmark Blog.

There is no scientific method for an item in your closet to become a Host Pick but there is a short-cut you can do to increase your odds. There are two ways to be aware of any upcoming Posh Party:

1) If your settings allow, you can get a notification of the Posh Parties to be held the following day

2) Go to "Shop", "All Parties"

To casually introduce Posh Party Hosts to your closet, follow the basics of the **Have a HEART** process.

25

Click on the Parties you are hoping to have a featured Host Pick. Be sure your listings that you believe are candidates to be a Host Pick are at the top of your closet. For example, if it's a Girls' Night Out Party you must have listings that fit into the theme at the top of your closet.

The hosts of the party will be listed. Simply click on each Hosts image and perform the "Target: Like / Follow / Share" step. You can even go a step further and bundle several of their products (but not purchase). It's the same philosophy of the rest of this book, the soon-to-be Host is likely going to take note of your activity on their page. Their most likely reaction will be to click on your closet. By following the **Have a HEART** process, an item that is perfect to be a Host Pick for their party theme will be right in front of them!

Unlike the other processes defined in this book, a Host one day prior to her show is going to be very busy. So this process is intended to increase your odds. I find that this takes less than 5 minutes a day so why not go for it to get a Host Pick now and then? A Host Pick doesn't guarantee sales but garners a lot of attention!

Sources

Poshmark Statistics:
http://expandedramblings.com/index.php/business-directory/19875/poshmark-com/

Made in United States
Orlando, FL
15 March 2025

59489766R00021